ReadyGEN®

Text Coll

GRADE

ISBN-13: 978-0-328-85795-1
ISBN-10:   0-328-85795-5

11 20

Predicting Change

Come On, Rain!

BY **Karen Hesse**   PICTURES BY **Jon J Muth**   5

"Come on, rain!" I say,

squinting into the endless heat.

Mamma lifts a listless vine and sighs.
"Three weeks and not a drop,"
she says, sagging over her parched plants.

The sound of a heavy truck rumbles past.
Uneasy, Mamma looks over to me.
"Is that thunder, Tessie?" she asks.
Mamma hates thunder. I climb up the steps
for a better look. "It's just a truck, Mamma," I say.

I am sizzling like a hot potato.
I ask Mamma, "May I put on my bathing suit?"
"Absolutely not," Mamma says, frowning
under her straw hat.
"You'll burn all day out in this sun."

Up and down the block,
cats pant,
heat wavers off tar patches
in the broiling alleyway.
Miz Grace and Miz Vera bend,
tending beds of drooping lupines.

Not a sign of my friends
Liz or Rosemary,
not a peep from my pal Jackie-Joyce.

I stare out over rooftops,
past chimneys, into the way off distance.
And that's when I see it coming,
clouds rolling in,
gray clouds, bunched and bulging
under a purple sky.

A creeper of hope circles 'round my bones.
"Come on, rain!" I whisper.

Quietly,

while Mamma weeds,

I cross the crackling-dry path
past Miz Glick's window . . .

. . . glancing inside as I hurry by.

Miz Glick's needle sticks on her phonograph,
playing the same notes over and over
in the dim, stuffy cave of her room.

11

The smell of hot tar and garbage bullies the air
as I climb the steps to Jackie-Joyce's porch.
"Jackie-Joyce?" I breathe, pressing my nose
against her screen.

Jackie-Joyce comes to the door.
Her long legs, like two brown string beans,
sprout from her shorts.
"It's going to rain," I whisper.
"Put on your suit and come straight over."

12

Slick with sweat,

I run back home and slip up the steps past Mamma.

She is nearly senseless in the sizzling heat,

kneeling over the hot rump of a melon.

In the kitchen, I pour iced tea to the top
of a tall glass.
I aim a spoonful of sugar into my mouth,
then a second into the drink.

"Got you some tea, Mamma," I say,
pulling her inside the house.

Mamma sinks onto a kitchen chair
and sweeps off her hat.
Sweat trickles down her neck
and wets the front of her dress
and under her arms.
Mamma presses the ice-chilled glass
against her skin.
"Aren't you something, Tessie,"
she says.
I nod, smartly.
"Rain's coming,
Mamma," I say.

Mamma turns
to the window
and sniffs.
"It's about time,"
she murmurs.

15

Jackie-Joyce, in her bathing suit,
knocks at the door, and I let her in.

"Jackie-Joyce has her suit on, Mamma," I say.
"May I wear mine, too?"

I hold my breath,
waiting.
A breeze blows the thin curtains into the kitchen,
then sucks them back against the screen again.

16

"Is there thunder?" Mamma asks.
  "No thunder," I say.
"Is there lightning?" Mamma asks.
  "No lightning," Jackie-Joyce says.
"You stay where I can find you," Mamma says.
  "We will," I say.
"Go on then," Mamma says,
  lifting the glass to her lips to take a sip.

"Come on, rain!" I cheer,
peeling out of my clothes and into my suit,
while Jackie-Joyce runs to get
Liz and Rosemary.

17

We meet in the alleyway.

All the insects have gone still.

Trees sway under a swollen sky,

the wind grows bold and bolder,

. . . and just like that,

rain comes.

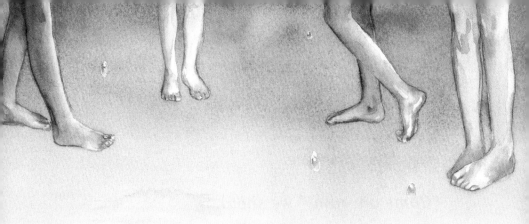

The first drops plop down big,

making dust dance all around us.

Then a deeper gray descends
and the air cools and the clouds burst,

and suddenly
rain is everywhere.

"Come on, rain!" we shout.

20

It streams through our hair and down our backs.
It freckles our feet, glazes our toes.
We turn in circles,
glistening in our rain skin.
Our mouths wide,
we gulp down rain.

Jackie-Joyce chases Rosemary

who chases Liz

who chases me.

Wet slicking our arms and legs,

we splash up the block,

squealing and whooping

in the streaming rain.

We make such a racket,
Miz Glick rushes out on her porch.
Miz Grace and Miz Vera come next,
and then comes Mamma.
They run from their kitchens and skid to a stop.

Leaning over their rails,
they turn to each other.
A smile spreads from porch to porch.
And with a wordless nod . . .

24

. . . first one, then all . . .

. . . fling off their shoes,
skim off their hose,
tossing streamers of stockings over their shoulders.
Our barelegged mammas dance down the steps
and join us in the fresh, clean rain . . .

26

. . . while the music from Miz Glick's phonograph

shimmies and sparkles

and streaks like night lightning.

Jackie-Joyce, Liz, Rosemary and I,

we grab the hands of our mammas.

We twirl and sway them,

tromping through puddles,

romping and reeling in the moisty green air.

We swing our wet and wild-haired mammas

'til we're all laughing

under trinkets of silver rain.

I hug Mamma hard,
and she hugs me back.
The rain has made us new.

> As the clouds move off,
> I trace the drips on Mamma's face.
> Everywhere, everyone, everything
> is misty limbs, springing back to life.

"We sure did get a soaking, Mamma," I say,
   and we head home
      purely soothed,
         fresh as dew,
            turning toward the first sweet rays of the sun.

30

EZRA JACK KEATS

THE SNOWY DAY

31

32

One winter morning Peter woke up
and looked out the window. Snow
had fallen during the night. It covered
everything as far as he could see.

34

After breakfast he put on his snowsuit and ran outside. The snow was piled up very high along the street to make a path for walking.

Crunch, crunch, crunch, his feet sank into the snow.

He walked with his toes pointing out, like this:

He walked with his toes
pointing in, like that:

37

Then he dragged his feet s-l-o-w-l-y
to make tracks.

And he found something sticking out
of the snow that made a new track.

It was a stick

— a stick that was just right for
smacking a snow-covered tree.

Down fell the snow —

plop!

— on top of Peter's head.

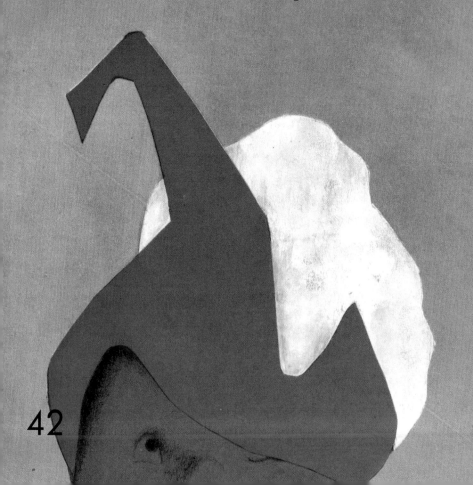

43

44

He thought it would be fun to join the big boys in their snowball fight, but he knew he wasn't old enough — not yet.

So he made a smiling snowman,

and he made angels.

He pretended

he was a mountain-climber.

He climbed up

a great big tall

heaping mountain of snow —

and slid all the way down.

He picked up a handful of snow — and another,
and still another. He packed it round and firm and
put the snowball in his pocket for tomorrow. Then
he went into his warm house.

He told his mother all about his adventures
while she took off his wet socks.

And he thought and thought
and thought about them.

53

Before he got into bed he looked in his pocket.

His pocket was empty. The snowball wasn't there.

He felt very sad.

While he slept, he dreamed that the sun had melted all the snow away.

But when he woke up his dream was gone.

The snow was still everywhere.

New snow was falling!

After breakfast he
called to his friend
from across the hall,
and they went out
together into the
deep, deep snow.

Spring Rain

by Marchette Chute

The storm came up so very quick
    It couldn't have been quicker.
I should have brought my hat along,
    I should have brought my slicker.

My hair is wet, my feet are wet,
    I couldn't be much wetter.
I fell into a river once
    But this is even better.

60

Listen

by Margaret Hillert

Scrunch, scrunch, scrunch.
Crunch, crunch, crunch.
Frozen snow and brittle ice
Make a winter sound that's nice
Underneath my stamping feet
And the cars along the street.
Scrunch, scrunch, scrunch.
Crunch, crunch, crunch.

Weather Together

by Lillian M. Fisher

There are holes in the clouds
   where the sun peeks through,
Patches of sky,
   scraps of blue.
It's raining rain
   and bits of ice
Bounce down like
   tiny grains of rice.
This weather together
   changes by the minute
And I can hardly wait
   to walk out in it!

Weather

by Meish Goldish

Weather is hot,
Weather is cold,
Weather is changing
As the weeks unfold.

Skies are cloudy,
Skies are fair,
Skies are changing
In the air.

It is raining,
It is snowing,
It is windy
With breezes blowing.

Days are foggy,
Days are clear,
Weather is changing
Throughout the year!

Text

Come On, Rain! by Karen Hesse, illustrated by Jon J. Muth. Text copyright © 1999 by Karen Hesse. Illustrations copyright © 1999 by Jon J. Muth. Reprinted by permission of Scholastic Inc.

The Snowy Day, by Ezra Jack Keats. Copyright © 1962 by Ezra Jack Keats. Used by permission of Puffin Books, a division of Penguin Young Readers Group, a member of Penguin Group (USA) Inc., 345 Hudson Street, New York, NY 10014. All rights reserved.

"Spring Rain," from *Around and About* by Marchette Chute. Copyright © 1957. Reprinted by permission of Elizabeth Hauser.

"Listen," by Margaret Hillert. Used by permission of the author, who controls all rights.

"Weather Together," by Lillian M. Fisher, who controls all rights.

"Weather," from *101 Science Poems and Songs for Young Learners* by Meish Goldish. Copyright © 1996 by Meish Goldish. Reprinted by permission of Scholastic Inc.

Illustrations
60 Maranda Maberry, **61** Susan Reagan, **62–63** Shelly Hehenberger